Flowers
in Love

Moniek Vanden Berghe

Flowers
in Love

Photography: Kurt Dekeyzer

A work of love

Bridal flowers will always fascinate florists and flower en-thusiasts. Time and again, professionals want to charm and astonish their brides with the most beautiful and original wedding bouquets. Designing floral decorations for someone to carry all day is a demanding but always a very rewarding task. In close consultation with the bride a piece is designed that not only fits her dress, but also matches and mirrors her personality. Often a bride has a very strong vision about the wedding procession. It's a florist's task to translate her vision and dreams into flowers.

Accessories such as hair pieces, boutonnières, flowers for the children, car decorations,... in line with the style of the bouquet make for an elegant and harmonious wedding pro-cession. This book also shows a same-sex marriage, here again the floral designs are adapted to match the individuality and style of both partners. All personal romances can find an adequate translation in the flowers for the big day.

In *Flowers in Love 3* we look at enthralling new designs and techniques. Be mesmerized by the beauty and elegance of natural materials: mysterious Vanda, precious Ranunculus and romantic roses and be astounded by the staggering ex-pressiveness of leaves, bark, ranks and seeds.
Flowers in Love 3 plays with colour and experiments with shapes and different ways to carry a bouquet, without being blind to practicality. Often a bride prefers an elegant Calla bouquet, a subtle and minimal design but with many pos-sible variations and personal expressions. The book also shows variations on the more traditional posies and round clutches, all-time favourites that will always be in fashion. Personally, I take most delight in a finished bouquet when I succeeded in fitting a natural element - or any material that may have caught my attention during a short walk or a stroll through the garden - into the design.

What distinguishes bridal work from any other floral piece is its delicacy and the meticulous craftsmanship needed to de-liver a high-standard piece. Bridal work is all about details and finishes and should be made-to-measure, otherwise it will lack depth and intensity. Every bridal bouquet is carefully and passionately composed by the florist, a challenging task but often very much appreciated by the wedding couple. There is no such thing as a standard wedding bouquet; a florist has to open his mind to the views and personalities of the soon to be wed and find inspiration in their personal love story.

I hope that this book shows my passion for bridal work and may enthuse and inspire many others.

Moniek Vanden Berghe

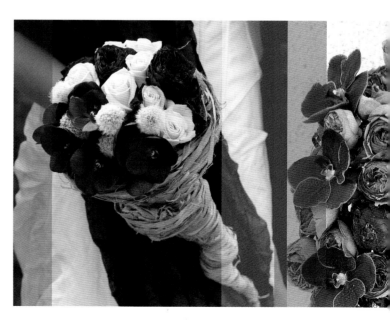

Passion for refined beauty

As editor of *Fusion Flowers* magazine I have found myself in the fortunate position of witnessing the development of floristry and I am ideally placed to witness the excesses of some and the tender exploration of others. However, once in a while there emerges a talent on the floristry stage that is so unique, so original and so remarkable, that its emergence has unwittingly affected international floral design for years to come, if not forever. In my opinion Moniek Vanden Berghe is one of these rare individuals. Without doubt the original *Flowers in Love* (2003) arrived at just the right time. For too many years bridal floristry had not taken into account current trends and was, to a certain extent, in text at least, dominated by male designers. Moniek proved that bridal floristry could, and should, take into account the dress, the human form, the taste of the individual concerned ... whilst still making a unique and personal connection with the bride herself. This ability is the mark of a truly gifted individual.

In previewing *Flowers in Love 3*, I was quite simply astounded as, once again, this highly artistic and very feminine lady has produced a collection of outstanding and original bridal concepts. The subject of good taste is subjective but it must be said; Moniek is quite simply incapable of creating anything that is not, in every sense of the term, exquisite taste. She has the ability to connect with the individual on a spiritual level through the use of flowers and her work shows the skill and dedication required to become what she effectively has become – a global trendsetter. We are fortunate indeed to have found her because she makes the world of flowers a richer, better place to be in and her books will inspire generations to come. *Flowers in Love 3* is quite simply – a triumph.

Alison Bradley

Un travail plein d'amour

Les fleurs de mariage continueront éternellement de fasciner fleuristes et passionnés. Les hommes et les femmes du commerce floral chercheront systématiquement à charmer et à étonner les futures mariées en leur confectionnant le plus merveilleux et original des bouquets. La création de compositions florales que quelqu'un porte sur soi pendant toute la journée, s'avère souvent délicate mais extrêmement enrichissante. Une composition se crée en étroite concertation avec la future mariée afin qu'elle puisse non seulement s'accorder à sa robe mais également refléter sa personnalité. De surcroît, les futures mariées ont souvent une vision exacte de leur cérémonie de mariage et l'interprétation de leurs rêves dans le langage des fleurs appartient au fleuriste.

Les accessoires de coiffure, les boutonnières, les fleurs destinées aux enfants, les décorations de voitures et autres ornements coordonnés au style du bouquet confèrent élégance et harmonie à toute la cérémonie. Cet ouvrage aborde en outre les mariages de même sexe pour lesquels les compositions florales doivent également s'adapter à l'individualité et au style de chaque partenaire. En effet, les fleurs du grand jour ont comme vertu de dresser une représentation fidèle de chaque romance personnelle.

Laissez *Flowers in Love 3* vous inspirer par ses charmantes compositions et techniques inédites. Laissez-vous éblouir par la beauté et l'élégance des fleurs naturelles telles que les mystérieuses orchidées Vanda, les précieuses renoncules ou encore les roses romantiques. Laissez-vous surprendre par l'expressivité renversante des feuilles, de l'écorce, des graines ou encore de l'agencement.
Flowers in Love 3 joue avec les couleurs et expérimente avec les formes et les différentes façons de porter un bouquet sans pour autant négliger le côté pratique. Les futures mariées préfèrent souvent l'élégance d'un bouquet de callas,

une composition minimaliste et subtile se prêtant toutefois à de nombreuses variations et personnalisations. Seront également présentées les nombreuses possibilités offertes par les petits bouquets et les bouquets boules : des coups de cœur intemporels !
Pour ma part, il n'est de meilleure satisfaction qu'un bouquet agrémenté d'une touche naturelle, ou de tout autre élément ayant attiré mon attention au cours d'une brève balade ou d'une promenade dans le jardin.

Les compositions florales de mariage se distinguent des autres bouquets par leur délicatesse et l'artisanat méticuleux dont elles résultent afin d'exhiber une classe supérieure. Reposant sur le goût du détail et des finitions, elles doivent être confectionnées sur mesure afin de ne manquer ni de constance, ni d'intensité. Chaque bouquet est composé avec soin et passion : un ouvrage délicat mais souvent très apprécié des futurs époux. Par ailleurs, il n'existe pas de composition de mariage standard, un fleuriste doit être réceptif aux attentes et aux personnalités des futurs mariés et puiser son inspiration dans leur histoire d'amour individuelle.

Je souhaite que cet ouvrage exprime ma passion pour les compositions florales de mariage et qu'il séduise et inspire de nombreux lecteurs.

Moniek Vanden Berghe

Une passion pour l'élégance

En tant qu'éditeur du magazine *Fusion Flowers*, je bénéficie d'une position privilégiée pour observer l'évolution de l'industrie florale et être témoin des excès de certains et de la délicate exploration des autres. Toutefois, de temps à autre, un talent émerge de la scène florale, tellement unique, original et remarquable qu'il va, à son insu, influencer la composition florale internationale pour des années à venir, sinon pour toujours. À mon avis, Moniek Van den Berghe est l'un de ces rares individus. Sans aucun doute, son ouvrage original *Flowers in Love* (2003) ne pouvait mieux tomber. Pendant de trop nombreuses années, la fleuristerie de mariage n'a su tenir compte des tendances actuelles et fut dominée, jusqu'à un certain degré, tout au moins par écrit, par des designers masculins. Moniek a prouvé que la fleuristerie de mariage pouvait et devait épouser la silhouette et la robe de la future mariée et s'imprégner de sa personnalité en établissant une connexion unique et individuelle avec elle. Ce type d'accomplissement est caractéristique d'une personne véritablement talentueuse.

Lors de ma première lecture de *Flowers in Love 3*, j'étais tout simplement étonnée car, une fois de plus, cette dame très féminine et artistique, a su produire une collection de compositions de mariage originales et remarquables. Même si le goût est affaire de sensibilité, cela mérite toutefois d'être dit, Moniek est tout simplement incapable de créer quelque chose qui ne soit pas, et dans tous les sens du terme, d'un goût exquis. Elle possède la capacité de se connecter aux individus sur le plan spirituel grâce aux fleurs. Son travail témoigne de ces compétences et de son dévouement indispensables pour devenir ce qu'elle est véritablement devenue, une instigatrice de tendances internationale. Nous avons en effet beaucoup de chance de l'avoir rencontrée car elle fait du milieu des fleurs, un monde meilleur, plus riche et ses livres inspireront bien des générations à venir. *Flowers in Love 3* est tout simplement - un triomphe !

Alison Bradley

Een werk vol liefde

Bruidsbloemen zullen floristen en bloemenliefhebbers altijd blijven fascineren. Steeds opnieuw willen vakmensen het mooiste, creatiefste en origineelste boeket voorstellen aan hun bruiden. Floraal werk creëren dat iemand een hele dag bij zich zal dragen is dan ook een hele bijzondere en dankbare opdracht. In overleg met de bruid wordt iets samengesteld dat alleen voor haar is ontworpen, dat niet alleen bij haar jurk maar ook bij haar persoonlijkheid aansluit en rekening houdt met specifieke voorkeuren en verlangens. Maar uiteraard houden we ook rekening met de smaak van de bruidegom.

Aangepaste accessoires zoals boutonnières, haartooi, bloemen voor de bruidskinderen, autodecoraties,... bepalen mee het harmonieuze beeld van de bruidsstoet. In dit boek tonen we ook een homohuwelijk, ook hier wordt gewerkt volgens de wensen en persoonlijke stijl van beide partners. Alle persoonlijke liefdesverhalen kunnen hun florale vertaling krijgen in het bloemwerk voor de grote dag.

In *Flowers in Love 3* zoeken we opnieuw naar vernieuwende technieken en boeiende ontwerpen. Laat u betoveren door de pracht en verfijning van natuurlijke materialen: mysterieuze Vanda's, schattige ranonkels en romantische rozen, en verbaas u over de verbluffende expressiviteit van bladeren, schors, ranken en peulen.
We spelen met kleuren, vormen en draagwijzen, maar het bloemwerk blijft altijd maakbaar en draagbaar. Vaak gaat de voorkeur van de bruid uit naar een eenvoudige bundel aronskelken, waarop verschillende creatieve variaties getoond worden, die weliswaar sober blijven maar wel telkens een persoonlijke toets krijgen. Er zijn ook talloze variaties op traditionele, ronde romantische boeketten, die altijd gewild zullen zijn.
Persoonlijk voel ik me het gelukkigst met een bruidsboeket als ik er een natuurlijk element in heb kunnen verwerken,

dat, al dan niet toevallig, op mijn pad kwam tijdens een kleine wandeling of een kort ommetje door de tuin.

Wat een bruidscreatie onderscheidt van ander bloemwerk is haar zorgvuldige afwerking. Bruidswerk is detailwerk en moet op maat gemaakt worden, zo niet mist het diepgang en intensiteit. Met passie, gedrevenheid en energie wordt het door de florist gecomponeerd, een uitdaging die veelal ten zeerste gewaardeerd wordt door het bruidspaar. Zich openstellen voor de wensen van het bruidspaar en inspiratie vinden in hun liefdesverhaal is dan ook een essentiële taak van de florist.

Ik hoop dat dit boek getuigt van mijn persoonlijke liefde en passie voor bruidswerk en velen mag inspireren.

Moniek Vanden Berghe

Passie voor verfijnde schoonheid

Als redactrice van *Fusion Flowers* magazine bevind ik me in een geprivilegieerde positie om de ontwikkelingen binnen de florale wereld op de voet te volgen, om de snelle opmars van sommigen en de voorzichtige stappen van anderen gade te slaan. Eens om de zoveel tijd verschijnt een bijzondere ster aan het floristieke firmament, een persoonlijkheid die zo uniek, origineel en opmerkelijk is dat haar verschijning een diepgaande, zo niet blijvende invloed zal hebben op de florale kunst. Naar mijn mening is Moniek Vanden Berghe een van die uitzonderlijke persoonlijkheden.

Flowers in Love (2003) kwam er net op het goede moment. Bruidsfloristiek werd jarenlang gedomineerd door mannelijke ontwerpers, was weinig vooruitstrevend en leek immuun voor trends die in de rest van de florale wereld succesvol hun opgang maakten. Moniek bewees dat bruidsfloristiek meer is dan een mooi boeket voor een bijzondere dag en afgestemd moet worden op de persoonlijkheid, de bijzondere wensen en verlangens van de bruid. Met bijzondere fijngevoeligheid en

kundige vingers vertaalt Moniek Vanden Berghe die dromen in stijlvolle boeketten. Dat is het kenmerk van echt talent.

Bij het inkijken van *Flowers in Love 3* werd ik getroffen door datzelfde gevoel. Opnieuw is deze grande dame erin geslaagd een uitmuntende, eigentijdse bruidscollectie samen te stellen. Goede smaak mag dan misschien subjectief zijn; Moniek Vanden Berghe is eenvoudigweg niet in staat om iets te creëren dat niet in elk opzicht getuigt van exquise smaak en overdonderende originaliteit. Haar bloemenkeuze en creaties getuigen van het technische meesterschap en de toewijding die Moniek hebben gemaakt tot wat ze effectief is – een global trendsetter. We hebben het geluk om haar in ons midden te hebben. Mogen haar boeken generatieslang mensen inspireren en moge *Flowers in Love 3* een nieuwe triomf zijn!

Alison Bradley

Calamus rotang
Vanda 'Mini Blue'
Vanda 'Royal Blue'

Calamus rotang
Vanda 'Mini Blue'
Vanda 'Royal Blue'

Oreopanax andreanus
Ozothamnus diosmifolius
Ranunculus asiaticus (hybrid)

↑

Tillandsia xerographica
Rosa 'Heaven'
Rosa 'Memory Lane'
Brunia laevis (Silver Brunia)

↑

Brunia albiflora
Calamus rotang
Echinoidea sp (sea urchin)
Ranunculus
Rosa 'Memory Lane'
Tillandsia xerographica

Begonia (rex group)
Daphne sp
Rosa 'Piano'
Rosa 'Vendella'
Taraxacum officinale
Vanda 'Violet Red Magic'

←

Anthurium 'Midori'
Anthurium 'Snowy'
Bromus sterilis
Liriope spicata
Paeonia 'Duchesse de Nemours'

← ←

Asparagus asparagoides
Lilium 'Casa Blanca'
Molucella laevis
Paeonia 'Duchesse de Nemours'
Scindapsus pictus

Corylus maxima 'Purpurea' (fruit)
Cotinus coggygria 'Royal Purple'
Rosa 'Piano'

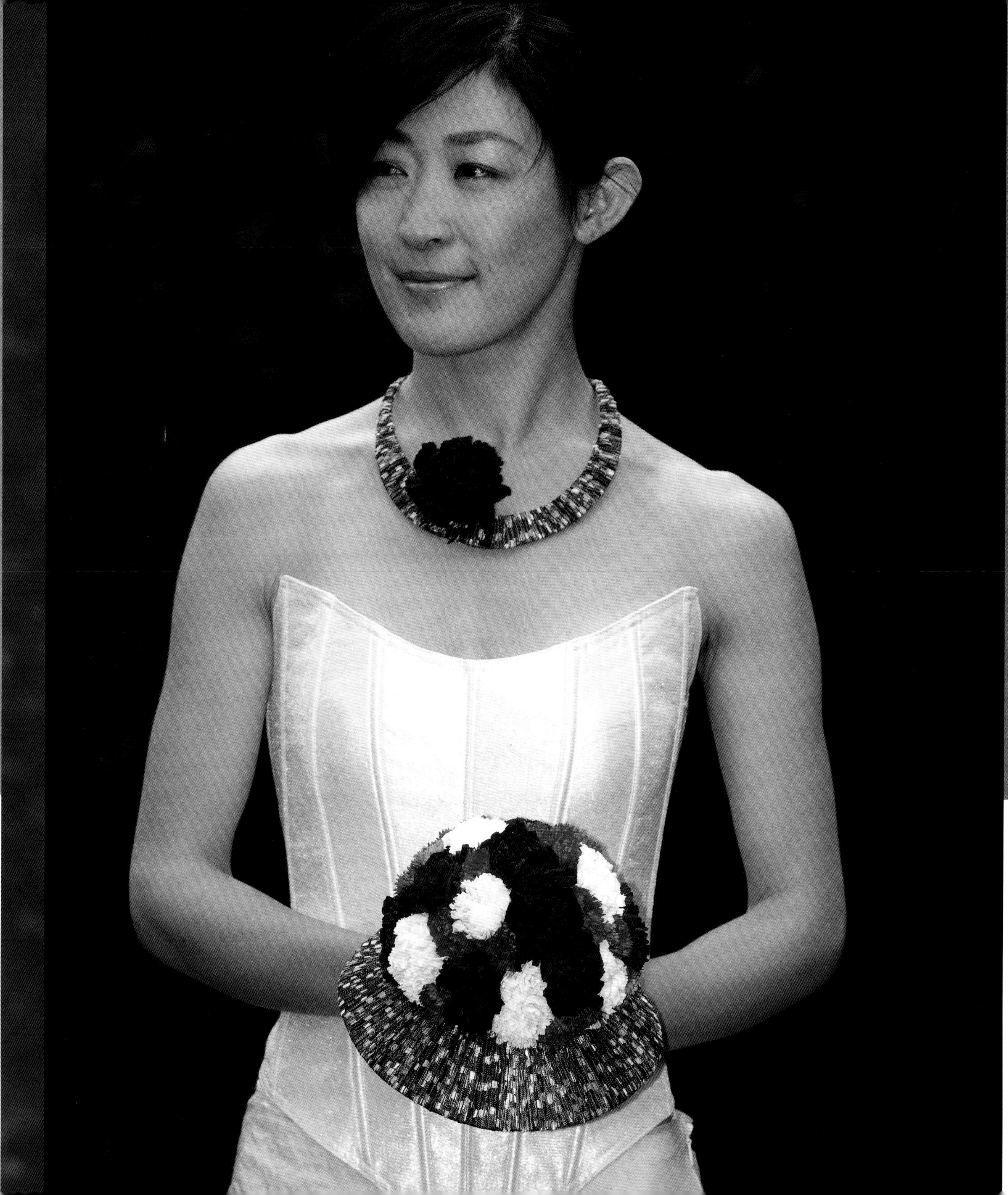

←
Ozothamnus diosmifolius
Ranunculus asiaticus (hybrid)

↑
Cyathea dealbata
Rosa 'Piano'
Stachys byzantina

← ←
Dianthus plumarius (hybrid)

→
Calamus rotang
Carex sp
Gerbera (Germini) 'Husky'

→→
Cryptanthus (hybrid)
Ranunculus asiaticus (hybrid)

↑
Ficus binnendijkii
Lysimachia ephemerum

←
Delphinium 'Völkerfrieden'
Liriope spicata

Gaultheria shallon
Ranunculus asiaticus (hybrid)
Viburnum opulus 'Roseum'

←
Dianthus plumarius (hybrid)
Germini 'Vigoury'
Rosa 'Finesse'

→
Allium 'Purple Sensation'
Daphne sp
Ranunculus asiaticus (hybrid)
Vanda 'Cerise Magic'
Vanda 'Orange Magic'

Anthurium 'Grace'

Anthurium 'Midori'

Anthurium 'White Love'

Bromus sterilis

Calamus rotang

Chrysanthemum (santini) 'Froggy'

Begonia (rex group)
Eriobotrya japonica
Ranunculus asiaticus (hybrid)

Betula pendula
Lilium longiflorum
Ranunculus 'Success Green'
Scindapsus pictus
Viburnum opulus 'Roseum'

→

←

Lunaria annua
Zantedeschia 'Green Goddess'
Zantedeschia 'Schwarzwalder'

←

Anthurium 'Midori'
Bromus sterilis
Chrysanthemum 'Feeling Green Dark'
Gentiana asclepiadea
Hydrangea macrophylla cv
Rosa 'F Green'

→
Bromus sterilis
Calamus rotang
Dianthus plumarius (hybrid)
Gentiana asclepiadea
Hoya carnosa f. compacta
Hydrangea macrophylla cv
Rosa 'Akito'

↑
Cotinus coggygria
Paeonia lactiflora cv
Raphia farinifera
Vanda 'Exotic Red'

← ←
Ranunculus 'Picotee'

←
Delphinium 'Völkerfrieden'
Ophiopogon planiscapus
Rosa 'F Green'
Trifolium ochroleucum

→
Agapanthus (hybrid)
Hydrangea macrophylla cv
Ophiopogon planiscapus
Paeonia 'Duchesse de Nemours'
Rosa 'F Green'
Trifolium ochroleucum

←

Vanda 'Springtime Blue'

→
Hydrangea macrophylla
'Schneeball'
Ligustrum (hybrid)
Rosa 'Grand Prix'
Vanda 'Royal Blue'

←
Cortaderia selloana
Craspedia globosa
Nymphaea alba
Stachys byzantinum

Begonia (rex group)
Craspedia globosa
Paeonia lactiflora (hybrid)
Vanda 'Yellow Magic'
Vitis vinifera

←
Anthurium 'White Love'
Chrysanthemum (santini) 'Country'
Salvia officinalis

→
Chrysanthemum (santini) 'Noki'
Oreopanax andreanus
Zantedeschia 'Crystal Blush'

←
Alnus glutinosa (catkins)
Ozothamnus diosmifolius
Paeonia 'Dr. Alexander Fleming'
Paeonia 'Kansas'
Paeonia officinalis
Rosa 'Augusta Louise'

→
Daphne sp
Rosa 'Piano'

←
Betula pendula
Ranunculus asiaticus (hybrid)
Rosa 'Vendela'
Vanda (hybrid)

→
Acacia
Clematis armandii
Cotinus coggygria
Rosa sp
Rosa 'Sandy'
Sandersonia aurantiaca
Vanda (hybrid)

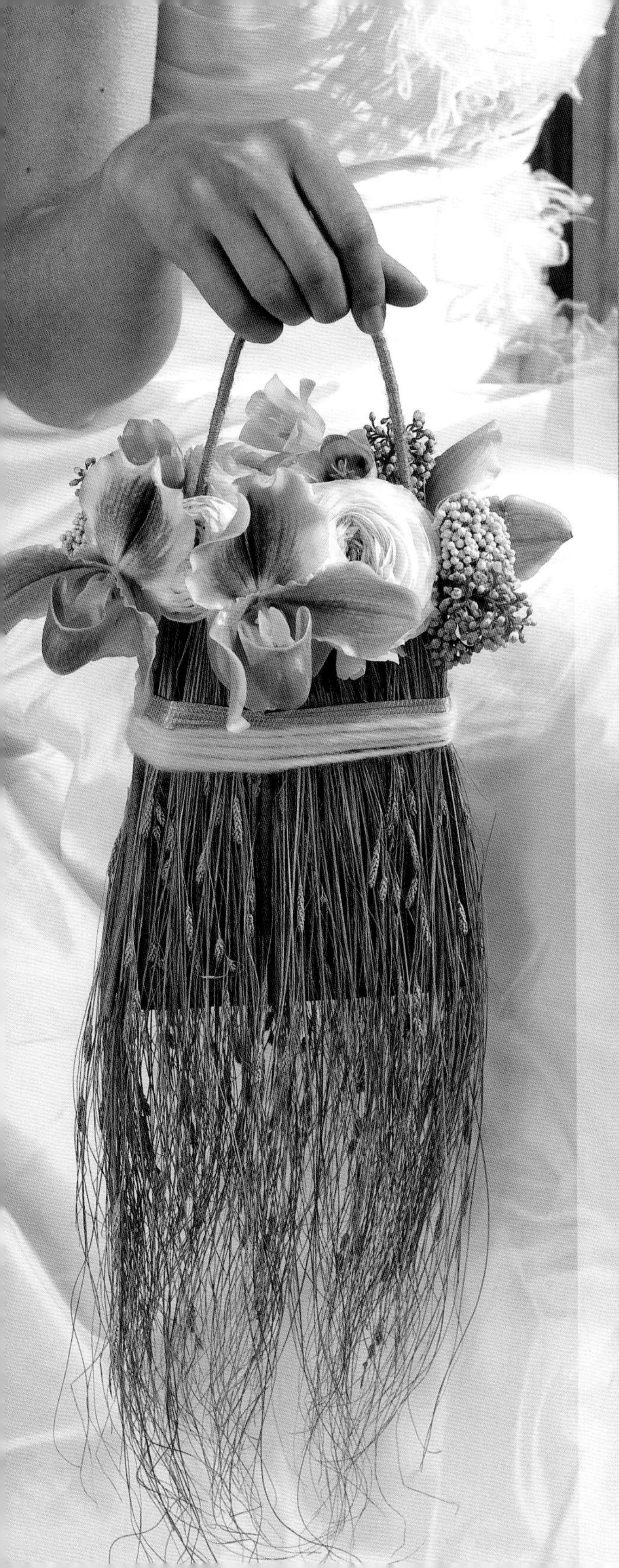

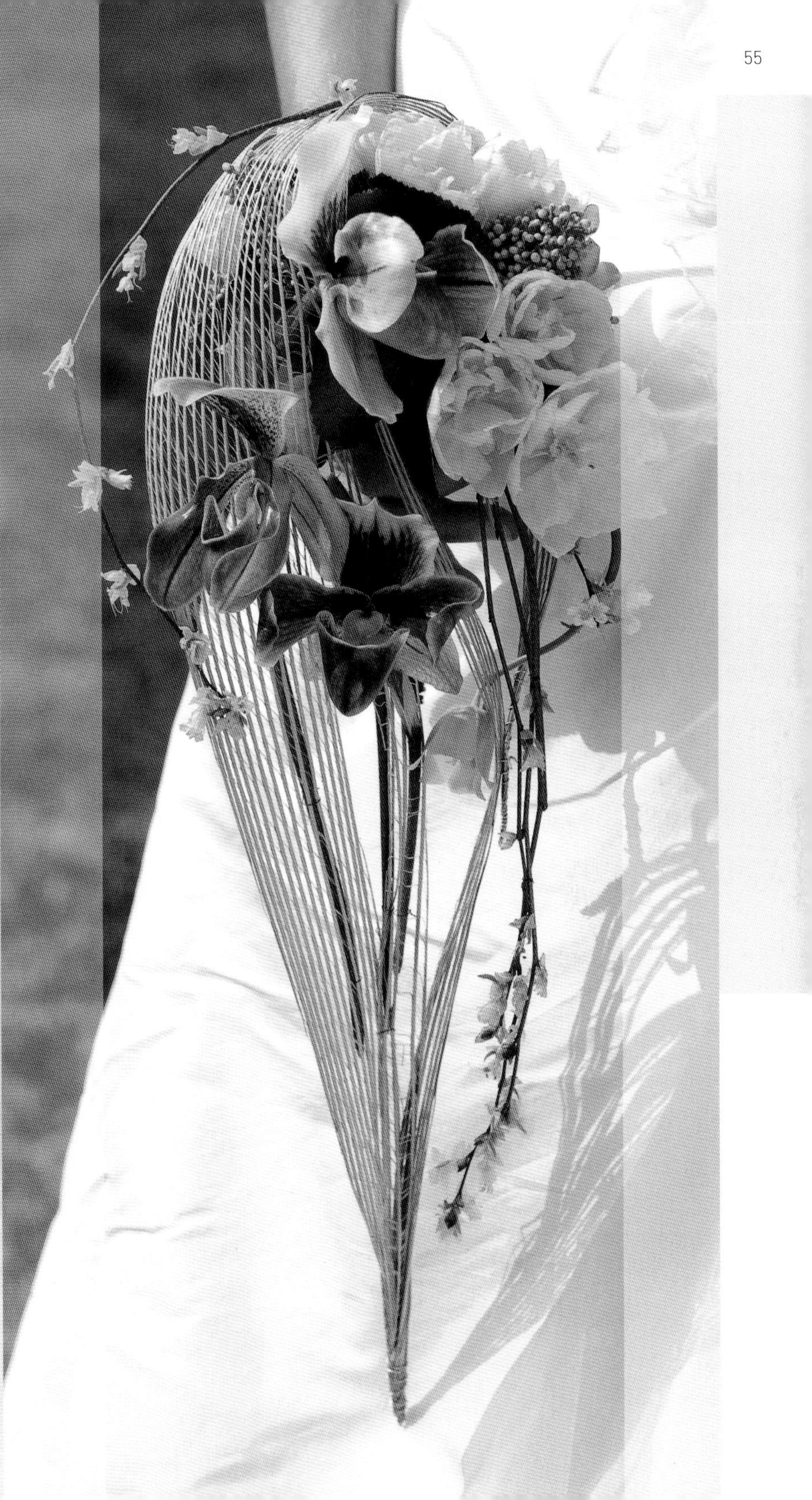

Calystegia sepium
Clematis vitalba
Cortaderia selloana
Hedera helix
Hydrangea arborescens 'Annabelle'
Miscanthus sinensis
Rosa 'Vendela'
Rosa 'Peach Avalanche'
Weigelia 'Minor Black'

Alnus glutinosa
Craspedia globosa
Daphne sp
Nymphaea alba
Ozothamnus diosmifolius

Vanda 'Exotic Purple'
Hydrangea macrophylla cv
Salvia officinalis
Taraxacum officinale

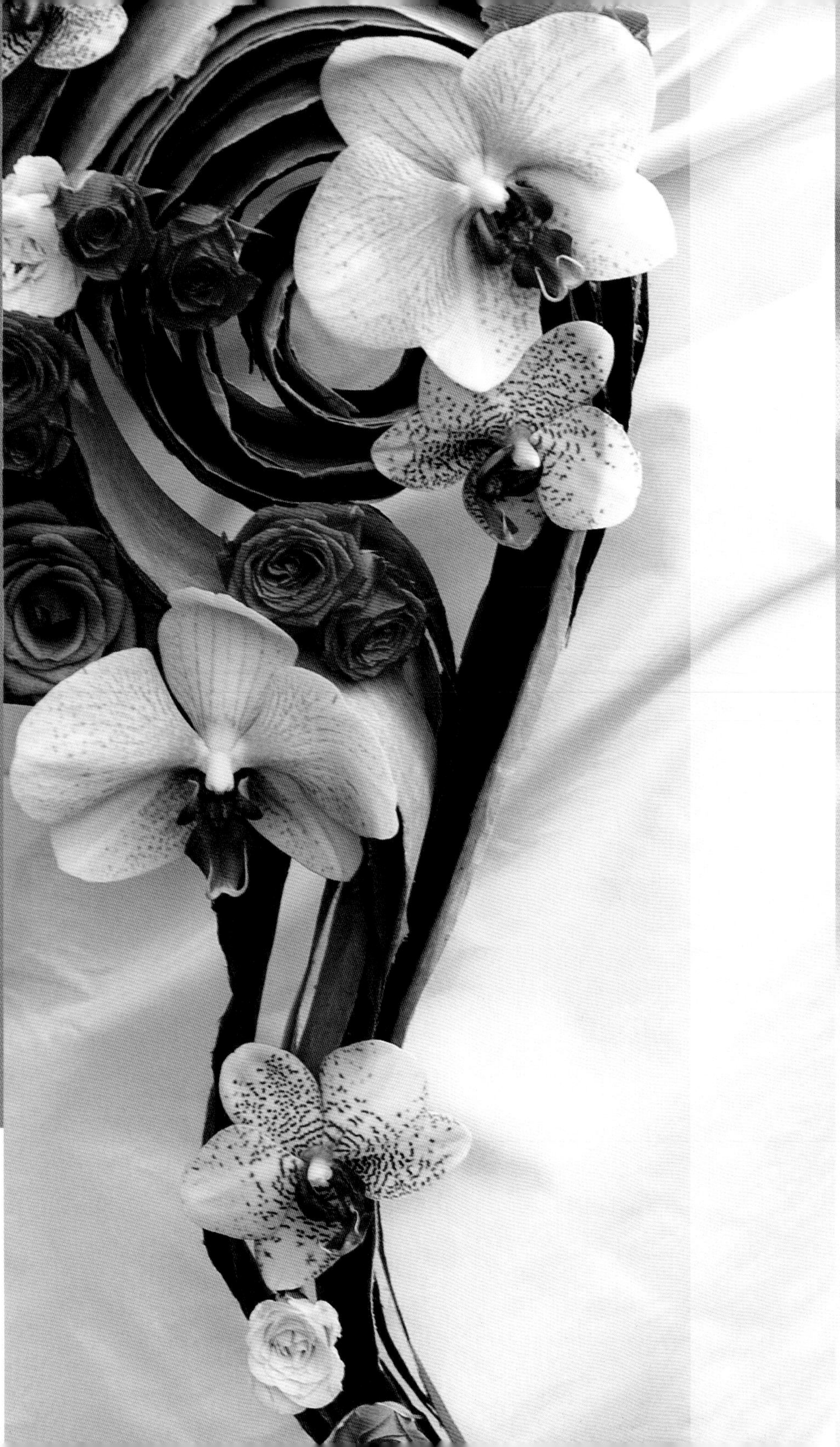

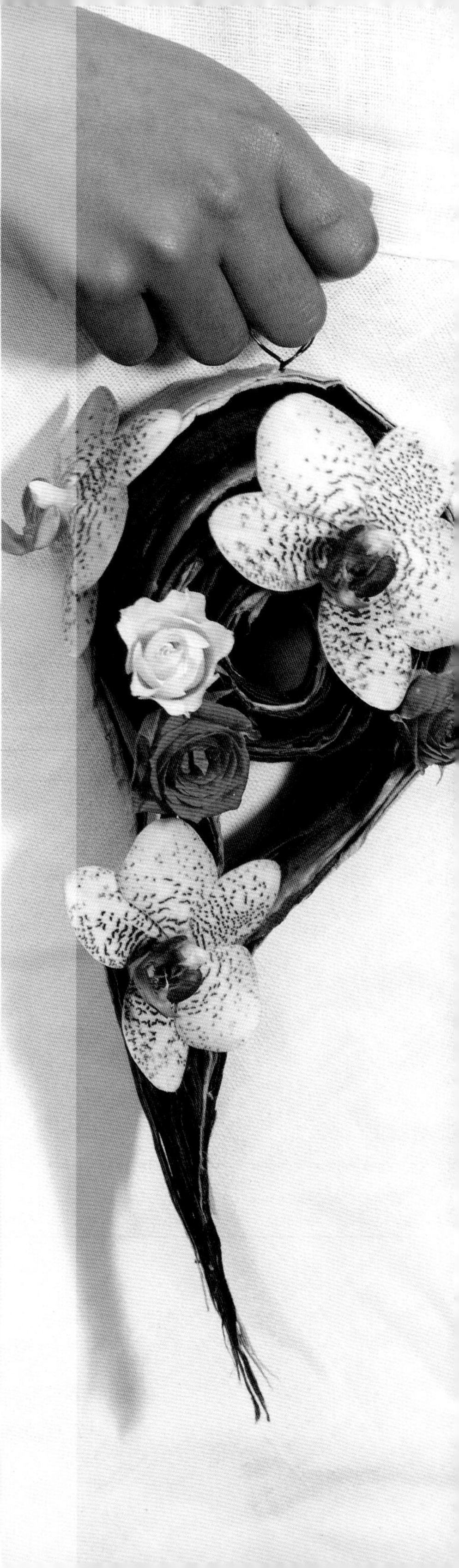

Phalaenopsis 'Omega'
Rosa 'Amalia'
Rosa 'Avantgarde'
Rosa 'Vendela'

Aspidistra elatior
Dianthus 'Green Trick'
Ranunculus asiaticus (hybrid)

Ranunculus asiaticus (hybrid)
Viola F1 (hybrid)

Vanda (hybrid)
Clematis tangutica
Cotinus coggygria 'Royal Purple'
Paeonia 'Garden Treasure' (Itoh-group)
Corylus maxima 'Purpurea'

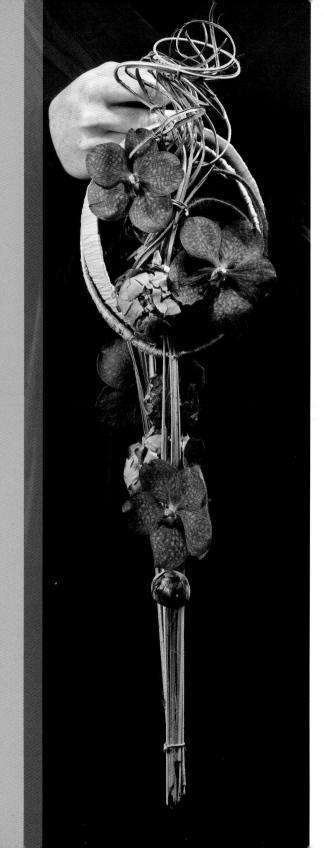

← Vanda 'Cerise Magic'
Paeonia lactiflora (hybrid)
Raphia farinifera
curly ting ting

→ Zantedeschia 'Vermeer'

Lunaria annua
Phalaenopsis

Heuchera micrantha 'Palace Purple'
Lonchocarpus
Miscanthus sinensis
Rosa 'Lydia'
Rosa 'Avantgarde'
Rosa 'Cool Water'
Rosa 'Vendela'
Vanda (hybrid)

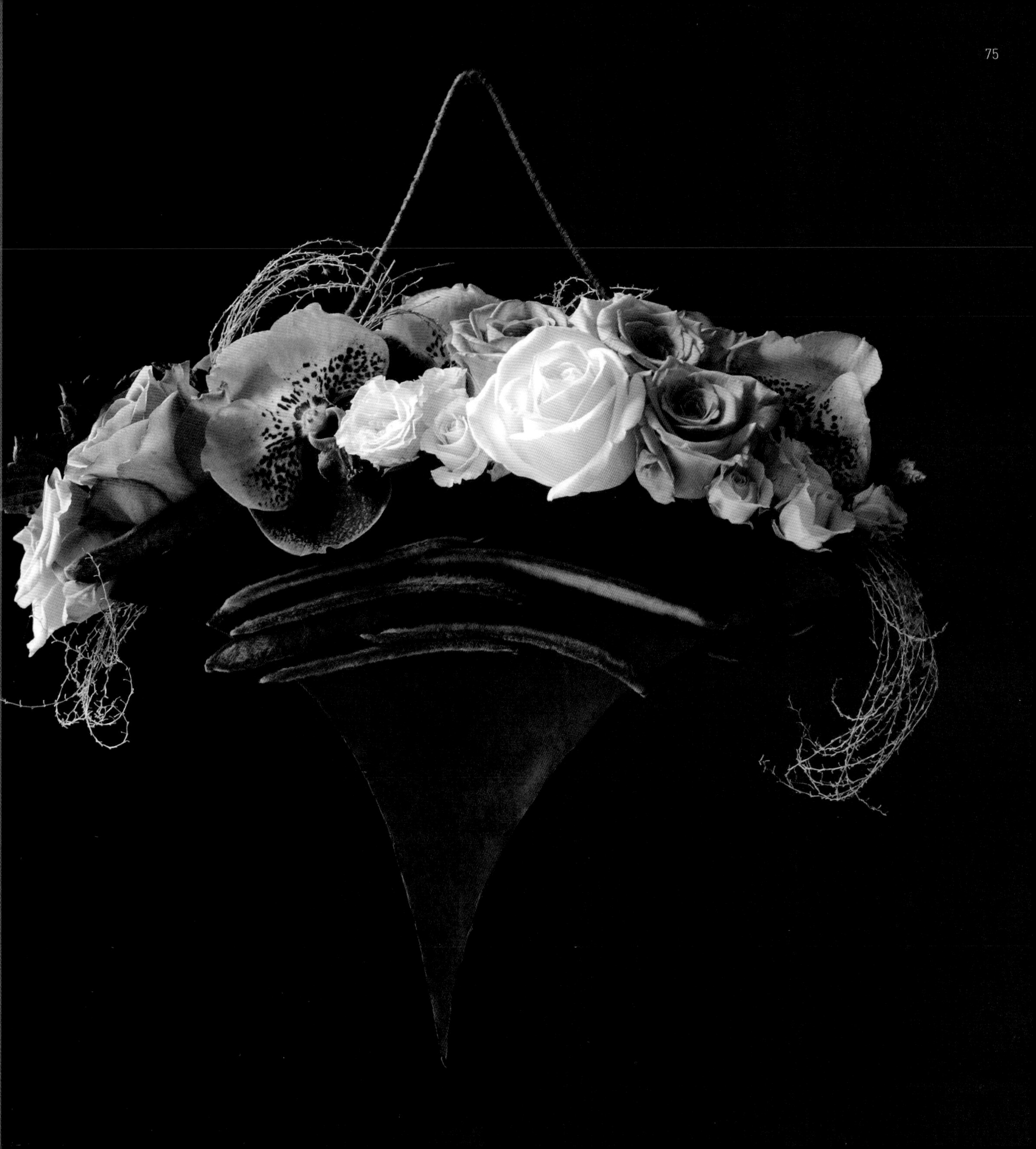

Heuchera micrantha 'Palace Purple'

Lonchocarpus

Miscanthus sinensis

Rosa 'Lydia'

Rosa 'Avantgarde'

Rosa 'Cool Water'

Rosa 'Vendela'

Vanda (hybrid)

Lilium longiflorum
Salix viminalis

↑
Aristea confusa
Tilia tomentosa
Vanda 'Dark Blue Magic'
Vanda 'Little Blue'

←
Lilium longiflorum
Salix viminalis

↑
Helleborus argutifolius
Lisianthus 'Minuet Dark Purple'
Oreopanax andreanus
Vanda 'Dark Blue Magic'
Viburnum opulus 'Roseum'

Vanda 'Fuchsia'
Vanda 'Pink Bordeaux Magic'
Vanda 'Pink Magic'

←
Ranunculus asiaticus (hybrid)
Viburnum opulus 'Roseum'

→
Oreopanax andreanus
Zantedeschia 'Crystal Blush'

→
Paeonia lactiflora (hybrid)
Ranunculus asiaticus (hybrid)
Rosa 'Avantgarde'
Viburnum opulus 'Roseum'
Zantedeschia 'Crystal Blush'

←

Anemone pulsatilla
Bromus sterilis
Cordyline australis
Hydrangea macrophylla cv
Ligustrum (hybrid)
Lunaria annua
Rosa 'Avantgarde'

Calamus rotang
Cordyline australis
Cotinus coggygria 'Royal Purple'
Dianthus barbatus
Heuchera micrantha 'Palace Purple'
Nectaroscordum siculum
Rosa 'Talea'

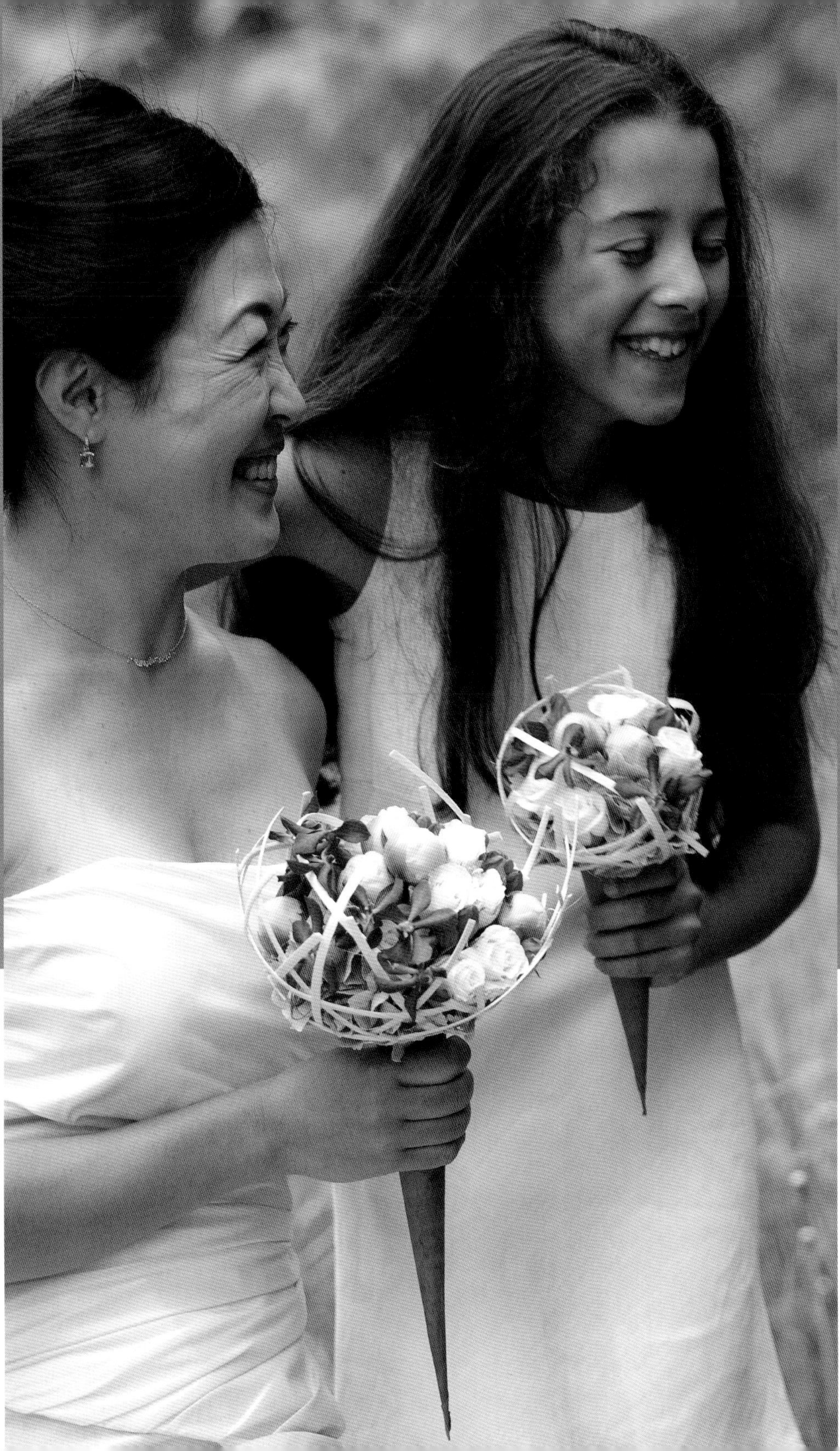

Calamus rotang
Gentiana asclepiadea
Hydrangea macrophylla cv
Paeonia 'Duchesse de Nemours'
Rosa 'Akito'
Vanda 'Mini Blue'

 Agapanthus (hybrid)
Bromus sterilis
Delphinium 'Völkerfrieden'
Lilium 'Casa Blanca'
Salix viminalis

Agapanthus (hybrid)
Gentiana asclepiadea
Hydrangea macrophylla cv
Rosa

Clematis tangutica
Zantedeschia 'Picasso'

Oreopanax andreanus
Vanda (hybrid)

↑
Paeonia officinalis
Raphia farinifera
Rosa 'Chippendale'
Vanda 'Bordeaux Magic'

←
Vanda 'Black Magic'

→
Peperomia rotundifolia
Vanda 'Mini Blue'

↑
Anthurium 'Midori'
Ophiopogon planiscapus

→
Dahlia (hybrid)
Lathyrus odoratus
Pisum sativum

Bromus sterilis
Dianthus 'Matrioska'
Lathyrus odoratus

↑
Clematis montana cv
Dianthus 'Apple Tea'
Rosa 'Yves Piaget'

↑
Bromus sterilis
Carex acutiformis
Paeonia 'Duchesse de Nemours'
Pulsatilla vulgaris

Dianthus 'Green Trick'
Hydrangea macrophylla cv
Lunaria annua
Paeonia 'Duchesse de Nemours'
Viburnum opulus 'Roseum'

↑
Bromus sterilis
Lathyrus odoratus
Nephrolepis sp
Rosa ʹF Greenʹ
Rosa ʹMarroussiaʹ
Viburnum opulus ʹRoseumʹ

Betula pendula
Chrysanthemum 'Kiev'
Chrysanthemum 'Kiev Orange'
Ligustrum (hybrid)
Vanda 'Orange Magic'
Vanda 'Thai Peach'

Cocos nucifera
Ranunculus asiaticus (hybrid)
Vanda 'Sandy'

→
Daphne sp
Rosa 'Blush' (freeze-dried)

My heartfelt thanks to:

Kurt – for the many years of good teamwork and excellent cooperation.
You are a virtuoso in finding the right light and perfect angle.
Ward – for the tremendous efforts and technical creativity,
for your encouragement and warm presence.
Family – for your kind support, understanding and interest.
Friends – you are treasured and vital in my life.
Colleagues – working and thinking with you is a never-ending
source pleasure and inspiration.
My incredible assistants – Haruko Noda, Claire Caulier, Bart Van Didden,
Ferras Essa, Trees, Ann and Sandy
My teacher – Marc Derudder
Christel Boone – designer of bridal gowns and formal wear.

Our models:

Claire, Haruko, Cassandre, Liesbet, Tiffany, Liesbeth, Ferras, Jamesson,
Fee, Charlotte, Liesbeth and Wim, Benny and Kurt, Timpa

Also:

Harry van Trier, botanical expert
Alison Bradley, Fusion Flowers Magazine
Steef Van Adrichem, Anco orchids
Frans Moens, Avalane
Axel en Serge Vanden Bossche, Frank lambert, Serax-Maison d'être
Ellen Piessens, Marc Lust, Alexander De Boutte ao, Serax-Maison d'être
Bjorn Mervilde, Kristof Musschoot, Godshuis St Laureins: www.godshuis.be
Henri Clijsters, Chris Martens, Jan Joris, Stephen Short, Smithers-Oasis
The dedicated team at Stichting Kunstboek Publishers
Family Hemschoote, Rekad Publishers
Hugo Hendriks, Florever
Igor Chistrakov, Designerbooks: www.designerbooks.ru
Mr and Mrs Dhavé
Mr and Mrs Strobbe
Mr and Mrs Meersschaert
Mr and Mrs Vander Eecken
Mr and Mrs Boone
Mr and Mrs Speeckaert - Liebrecht
Mr and Mrs Maes - Van Renterghem
Mr and Mrs De Cabooter - Sierens
Gert Van Turnhout, Katty Proost, Kurt Van Dam, Dirk Laeremans, Luc Pauwels,
Dirk De Winter, Dirk Van Den Eynde ao, Agora-group
Family De Bleecker, Euroflor
Bart De Rijcke and assistants, Dora Flora
Kris Dimitriadis, Peter de Jaegher, Anne Denivel, Micha Vandormaal,
Geert Vrancken, PSG

Moniek Vanden Berghe

Training: floristry, IMOV, Gent.
Teacher Marc Derudder
Demonstrations in Belgium, the
Netherlands, Germany, Scotland, UK,
Ireland, France, USA, Japan, Australia,
Finland, Mexico, Korea.

Kurt Dekeyzer

Photography at the VZH in Hasselt (laureate)
Founder of Photo Studio Graphics (PSG),
a full-service bureau with own photo
studio and design department.

From left to right:
Kurt, Moniek & Ward

Previously published by the same author

Flowers in Love
ISBN 978-90-5856-161-9

Flowers in Love 2
ISBN 978-90-5856-224-1

Flowers in Tears
ISBN 978-90-5856-268-5

Creations / Créations / Creaties
Moniek Vanden Berghe
Gravin Mad. d'Alcantaralaan 120
B-9971 Kaprijke (Lembeke)
Tel.: +32 477 68 52 77
E-mail: cleome@telenet.be
Internet: www.cleome.be

Photography / Photographies / Fotografie
Kurt Dekeyzer, PSG
Heidestraat 18
B-3470 Kortenaken
Tel.: +32 11 22 09 95
E-mail: kurt.dekeyzer@psg.be

Kris Dimitriadis, PSG: p 49, 55, 57, 70, 87, 105
Kurt Deruyter: p 12, 64-65, 75, 92-93, 99 (detail), 100, 112-113
Florever: p 87

Co-ordination / Coordination / Coördinatie
Karel Puype
Katrien Van Moerbeke

Text / Textes / Tekst
Alison Bradley
Moniek Vanden Berghe

Final editing / Rédaction finale / Eindredactie
Katrien Van Moerbeke

Traduction française
Taal-Ad-Visie, Brugge

Layout & Print / Mise en pages & impression /
Vormgeving & druk
Group Van Damme bvba, Oostkamp

Published by / Une édition de / Een uitgave van
Stichting Kunstboek bvba
Legeweg 165
B-8020 Oostkamp
Tel.:+32 50 46 19 10
Fax: +32 50 46 19 18
E-mail: info@stichtingkunstboek.com
Internet: www.stichtingkunstboek.com

ISBN 978-90-5856-337-8
D/2010/6407/4
NUR 421